OLDER & HAPPIER!

INSPIRING, AMUSING, AND USEFUL ADVICE FOR MEN OF A CERTAIN AGE

DAG SEBASTIAN AHLANDER

TRANSLATED BY VERONICA CHOICE

Skyhorse Publishing

In memory of my grandfather Erik Tham,
a truly happy old man

Skyhorse Publishing books may be purchased in bulk at
special discounts for sales promotion, corporate gifts,
fund-raising, or educational purposes. Special editions
can also be created to specifications. For details, contact
the Special Sales Department, Skyhorse Publishing, 307
West 36th Street, 11th Floor, New York, NY 10018 or info@
skyhorsepublishing.com.

Skyhorse® and Skyhorse Publishing® are registered
trademarks of Skyhorse Publishing, Inc.®, a Delaware
corporation.

www.skyhorsepublishing.com

10 9 8 7 6 5 4 3 2 1

Library of Congress Cataloging-in-Publication Data is
available on file.

ISBN: 978-1-62873-646-5

Printed in China

109 HANDY IDEAS
FOR LIVING
LIFE TO THE FULLEST

A FEW YEARS AGO I RETIRED after working for 39 years, 11 months, and 7 days, which included seven exciting years as the Swedish Consul General in New York. Now, the time I have left is all mine. It's time for some real *after work*.

I am completely happy. Happy to finally have a chance to make decisions about my own life and my time and happy to take advantage of the powers within that I have not yet spent. According to statistics, I'm supposed to have another sixteen years to live, but you never know. So it's best to take advantage of each and every day.

Set on becoming a happy old man, on making the most of the home stretch, I took an inventory of all the positive experiences I've had in my life. It proved to be a valuable exercise. I found myself both surprised and delighted as I realized that life really had been good to me. First and foremost: I am happily married to the love of my life and we have two bright, young daughters who have both recently married their American sweethearts. One family lives in New York and the other in Stockholm; this is especially lucky, as I consider both to be my hometowns.

I have come a long way since I was born in the little university town of Uppsala, Sweden, in 1944. In 1955, my family moved to Washington, DC, where my father served for three years as a cultural attaché at the Swedish Embassy. In my own adult life as a Swedish diplomat, I have worked and lived in Moscow, Nairobi, Geneva, St. Petersburg, and New York. When I ended my career, I was an Ambassador with the Swedish State Department. Thanks to the path my work led me on, I had the opportunity to experience on site in Leningrad/ St. Petersburg our generation's biggest historical event: the collapse of communism in the Soviet Union and the Baltic Independence—all of it happening right next door to Sweden. That was my life's big adventure. And, after that, my family and I got to experience New York during the wonderful '90s when all curves shifted upward. It was in this creative environment I started to write.

PERHAPS YOU THINK this account sounds light-hearted, and if so, you're right. As I warned you: You have to highlight the best parts and forget about the rest. Doing so is the only way to become a happy old man. You have to embrace your destiny and reshape the things that can still be changed. Magnify that which brings you joy and take pleasure in everyday life. I *want* to be happy and through that attitude alone, I think I am already halfway there.

Happiness is having a talent for destiny. This talent is something we have to try to cultivate later in life. Now it's your turn to take stock of all the wonderful things that have happened in your life!

Taking stock of your life in this way inevitably leads to a certain degree of self-righteousness. You probably think I sound pretty self-satisfied right about now. It's unavoidable: I am my own guinea-pig for the approach outlined in this book. I don't think it's so strange that I am happy and proud to acknowledge the difficulties I have managed to overcome, and that I want to share what I have learned in the process. That's the very purpose of this little book of advice.

That being said, I don't always manage to follow my own advice. I fail all the time! But at least now I know when I've made a mistake and have to start all over again. By recognizing your own error, you've already come a long way.

AND ALL OF A SUDDEN WE ARE STANDING ON THE OPPOSITE SHORE

RETIREMENT IS THE last big shift in life. It's also the last big challenge. Knowing how to live was so much easier when the future was ahead of us. Now, it's harder, because none of us have ever been old before.

Old age isn't a stage of development, but rather one of decline. This makes it even more of a challenge. We have to keep striving, even though we know how the story ends. This is precisely why we need a good sense of humor as we age, and why it's so important to be happy as old men.

There is much to be happy about. With each generation, we live longer and stay healthier. In Sweden, the life expectancy for men is now 79 years and 10 months and for women it is 83 years and 2 months. In the US it's slightly lower (76 for men, 81 for women).

We are also reaching "old age" much later than our parents and grandparents did. Today's 75 is yesterday's 65. At 65, many of us still have a third of our lives left to live. That's not bad!

BUT FIRST WE HAVE to resolve a few things that befell many men of our generation and that are preventing them from becoming truly happy old men. Men born in the 1940s and '50s found their career plans crossed by women's movement into the workplace. This meant the competition for work increased. Many employers were actively seeking the female alternative. Because of this, about half of the number of jobs that were traditionally appointed to men vanished to them. The result was better equality between men and women and a better society for all, but the individual men stuck in the transition did not always perceive it as such. That situation was and still is rarely discussed. Indeed, it has almost become a taboo subject; after all, we are proud of our society's evolution.

At the same time that the women's movement took hold, traditional hierarchies dissolved; secretaries, clerks, and people in similar types of jobs suddenly had new career opportunities, further changing the traditional career ladders. Plus, computerization led to more jobs becoming stationary and repetitive. Often, promotions only meant a heavier workload and more problems.

Because of this, many older men today are upset that their lives did not turn out the way they had wanted. This is the inevitable result of pervasive political and social movements in our time. While these movements were perfectly just and reasonable, many men experienced them as unfair. The ebbs and flows of any zeitgeist are inscrutable to its contemporaries.

I was personally affected at the age of 55 when I found my job opportunities shrinking as my boss, the Minister for Foreign Affairs, openly stated that she no longer had an interest in promoting men of my age. It was tough, yes. But I was fortunate enough to be able to turn this setback to an advantage by focusing instead on my writing.

While it may have been difficult for me personally, I do support these changes in society. I am a father of two daughters, and my daughters are now thriving young women with rewarding careers. And my wife, who had put her own professional life on hold for several years to follow me in my career, was given fantastic job opportunities of her own.

Remember that while life is lived moving forward, it can only be understood looking back. This is why the only thing we can do is continue moving forward while turning the next step in life to our advantage.

THE OTHER BIG CHANGE that occurred during our lifetime is the public sector's striking decrease in status as compared to the '60s. To be a government employee was once a highly prestigious position. The public sector was where the big reforms took place, and this was where power was concentrated during those peak years when society was restructured. Just think of the Kennedy Administration and the early years of the Johnson Administration. These are all reasons why so many people born in the '40s and '50s were drawn to the public sector.

But all of us who became executives during the '90s realized that government resources had run out and all that was left for us were cutbacks and reduced spending. We had to work harder than our predecessors ever did. And, in the computerized age, we had to do almost everything ourselves.

What's more, baby boomers grew up with the ideology that it was in the workplace that we were supposed to find both self-fulfillment and friends. We were also supposed to be active members of clubs, local communities, schools, unions, and churches. But that equation never quite tallied.

Now that we're older, we know better. On their deathbed, very few people complain about not having spent more time at the office. Usually it's the complete opposite. Too little time was dedicated to family, children, and friends and all of a sudden life had passed us by. Now that our professional lives have tapered off, we will find out whether our personal networks are in order.

Everything ends up meaning something in retrospect if we're open to certain reexamination. These days, being an entrepreneur and building your own business is the hot thing to do; the salaryman is no longer the obvious ideal. There are no longer as many preconceived notions about what is considered "proper"—in work and in life. This makes choosing more difficult, but it can also make life easier—even for us older folks. I am the diplomat who became the storyteller, and at this time, I have published twelve historical biographies for young readers. My teenage daughters became my editors, and in this way writing became our family's great father/daughter project.

Most of us can expand our interests and actualize our dreams after retirement. For many of us, this may lead to a new life—one *more* life to live. That is, essentially, the core message of this book.

The best compliment I've received in my new life happened in a school. As an author, I was invited to speak to an eighth grade class in a disadvantaged neighborhood. I talked about my books and spoke a little bit about my background. After the session, I was surprised to find myself surrounded by several boys asking questions about my books. Suddenly one boy asked, "How do I become like you?"

I will never forget that.

Remember that you can train yourself to enjoy life. We have to live our lives now—or never. There's no more time to procrastinate or to lament why life didn't turn out the way you had hoped. *This* is finally the time we can travel without a briefcase or read without writing a report. We don't have to constantly achieve or compromise and we don't have to keep seeking consensus. Now we can finally just . . . enjoy. I actually felt older back then than I do now!

And so, live a new life. Fulfill your own expectations, not those of others. Keep looking forward and you'll keep developing. The road doesn't exist until we walk it. This is what this book is all about.

I'VE SPENT MY LIFE in both Sweden and the United States, and I believe that the differences between the Swedish and the American way of life can offer new insight into how to become the happiest old men we can be.

I witnessed this difference in views on life when I moved to New York and needed to find an American doctor. Before the move, my Swedish doctor had given me a complete physical, along with every test imaginable.

"You are the healthiest fifty-year-old I have ever met," he said, which made me very happy to hear.

But after my new American doctor had performed the same tests and read my results his expression turned to one of concern.

"Consul General, you have a problem," he said.

Of course I was worried! When I related to him what my Swedish doctor had told me six weeks earlier, he replied:

"New York is a very stressful city."

He then asked me to send him the Swedish results, which I did. As it were, the test results turned out to be exactly the same. He looked puzzled. Then he said:

"Oh, I forgot that you're European."

Surprised, I asked him what he meant by that. He answered that in the United States the standard to which you compare all charts is a healthy twenty-year-old.

No wonder he found my results concerning! A fifty-year-old cannot have results comparable to a twenty-year-old, no matter how healthy, and I pointed this out.

The doctor begrudgingly agreed to my point of view. He was, however, not thrilled to have his judgment questioned.

I finally opted to say something to brush it all off:

"Oh well, no matter what, we'll all die in the end anyway."

This is when the doctor straightened himself up and said with a serious tone of voice:

"For my patients, death is not an option!"

General Rules
of Conduct

1

PLAN YOUR RETIREMENT WELL IN ADVANCE

It may sound boring, but some planning is necessary in order to really enjoy your later years. When you do leave your job, you'll lose some of the context—and the handy office perks—that will allow you to shape your new "free" life in a pleasant way.

What's more, Western society makes a clear divide between people who are in the workforce and senior citizens, or those of us who have retired. In Sweden, where the retirement age is set at 65–67, a lot of doors close at a certain age. There aren't too many companies who want 65-plusers serving on their boards. But just before that, say at 60, you're a wise and valuable commodity. Take advantage of that and do as much as you can before you exit.

In the US, there's a bit more flexibility. Many are active in the workforce up until their eighties. But, even so, if your golden age plan includes a world outside your office, you need to start thinking about retirement today. You are your own Talent Management Consultant now.

When you finally do start your new "free" life, however, be sure not to plan everything in excessive detail. In the Western world, we tend to plan too much and live too little. This goes for both work and leisure. I've witnessed this during my own experience living in various countries around the world.

Therefore, I suggest you get a small, simple calendar to keep track of your activities—not a huge planner that divides up your days by the hour. Something simple is all you need. Mine is red so it's easy to find. Beware of electronic calendars! They easily become a chore in themselves and will steal too much of your precious time.

2

KEEP IN MIND THAT TIME IS SHORT BUT LIFE IS LONG

Don't complain that time passes too quickly. Rather, think about how long life really is. If you, like myself, were born in 1944, then both Hitler and Stalin were alive during our lifetimes. They were engaged in atrocious genocide. World War II was raging.

With this as a background, it's incredible how long we have lived and how much we have experienced. Modern society was developed during our lifetime. Think about all the comforts we've gained and delicacies we've enjoyed and all the exciting trips we've taken around the world. Our generation, which is now reaching retirement, is historically very lucky indeed. We've experienced the peak years!

To gain perspective on our lives, let us consider the year 1944 as a hinge; if we could fold our lives back in time from this point, our lives would stretch back to the 1870s. That was when my grandfather was born, Otto von Bismarck had united Germany, Rutherford B. Hayes was elected president of the United States, Alexander Graham Bell patented the telephone, and Sweden was one of the poorest countries in Europe.

If this is how much the world has changed over two lifespans, then surely a human life is long. If we go back one more lifespan, we end up during the Napoleonic wars! Think about that the next time you hear someone complaining that life is too short. Life is actually so long that you even grow tired of thinking about death. That's been my experience, at least.

So, life isn't what's short. It's the remainder of your time that's short, which is another thing altogether. This means you have to grab hold of your life right now and make something great of what's left. The road doesn't go on forever and now we're on the homestretch. I may be ahead of you, but you'll definitely follow.

Since everyone who has lived before us has died, I'm not afraid of death. What I worry about is how it all will end. Because the truth is, we're not all equal in the face of death. Some die peacefully in their sleep, while others pass on after years of pain and suffering. Genes are all that count in the final stretch, which puts us back once again in the hands of our parents. We're adults, and yet we are no longer in control of our own lives. And there's nothing fair about it.

"Let's just hope that time proves to be a friend by moving slowly," as my friends in Kenya used to say.

3

FIRST AND FOREMOST: BE A HAPPY OLD MAN!

As the time for my retirement drew closer, my first decision was to try my best to become a happy old man. Optimists enjoy life much more than pessimists, even though life will eventually come to an end for us all.

The most important thing to do is to accept your age and enjoy its—honest to goodness—many opportunities. When getting older, everything depends on your attitude—even your health. Not all wines turn sour, nor do all people. Some improve with age! This is nothing new. As early as two thousand years ago, the Roman statesman and philosopher Cicero wrote:

"Life has its set road and nature is a one-way ticket. Every part of life has its own character so that the child's weakness, the stubbornness of the young and the more stable seriousness of maturity and the ripening of age is something natural that should be experienced in its own time."

His conclusion was: "The harvest of maturity is the rich memories of all the great things we have experienced in our lifetime."

The purpose of these quotes is not to show off, but rather to prove that throughout history intelligent people have contemplated the very same problems you and I are facing right now. When I was in school, I kept a journal of such thought-provoking quotes from which I still draw; they might not be verbatim, but they still get the message across. Let us take advantage of these combined experiences. Doing so has certainly made me more stoic, and perhaps that is where wisdom begins—who knows?

Put simply, the questions we are asking now are not new. Every person who came before us has died. There is a sense of comfort in that as well.

This is why you should begin each morning by greeting that old man in the bathroom mirror with a smile. It's time to like who you've become, even if you feel like a lost child behind the mask. The curious thing about growing old is that you live with all these ages inside you at the same time. If I look carefully enough in the mirror I can still see the carefree young schoolboy I once was.

There must be something positive in that. Perspective expands. I am a human like all those who have lived before me, and I, with my many selves, am a part of all that humanity. If we understand that, we have become just a little bit wiser. It's time to expound on that wisdom.

Always greet your neighbors with a smile, whether you're meeting at home, on the street, or at the store. I spend my summers with my family in a little fishing village in Skåne in the south of Sweden; here, everyone greets one another with a cheerful smile—except for some sour city slickers, of course. Smiles tend to be contagious, so go ahead and try to smile your way through life!

No, I don't want to be a whiny old man (which seems frighteningly easy) or just a plain boring old man (which seems to be most common). Nor do

I want to become one of the many old men who cling to their youth by trying to disguise their age with deep tans, young women, face lifts, make-up, and clothes designed for twenty-year-olds. Your lost-looking eyes in the line at the nightclub, in the crowds at that raucous bar, and under the shimmering disco ball will only reveal your true age—and it will do so mercilessly. In Roman comedies, the lovelorn old man is always the butt of all jokes, because through his ridiculous actions, he loses both his wisdom and his dignity. And after all, these are the greatest gifts of old age.

"To every thing there is a season, and a time to every purpose under the heaven: A time to be born, and a time to die [. . .] A time to weep, and a time to laugh," declared the preacher in the Old Testament more than three thousand years ago. It's just as true today.

A lot of anxiety disappears when we accept life's terms and make the best of them. When we do, there are no more Monday blues or dark November days. Every day we have left becomes valuable. I want to be living in harmony with my age, rather than always fighting against it. And to perhaps grow a little wiser. This is what my advice is all about.

It also seems as though we're perfectly placed in time. If you follow trends in fashion magazines, you'll notice that the trendy thing to do right now is celebrate "vintage" and "old ladies": Sheath dresses in floral print, home cooking, oven mitts, brewed coffee, cookies, traditional recipes, golden oldies. The old man ideal is "in" too. My daughters admire my round, horn-rimmed glasses—which I've been wearing for years! My friend, you're already a hipster; you don't even have to try (or grow an ironic beard). So let's embrace the passing of time, because sooner or later we'll be in vogue again.

The decision to become happy in my old age means that a certain sense of peace has settled through me. I used to think life was a bell curve, but now I feel as though I've inverted it. My life is turning upward again, not downward. My soul soars. I've gained clarity and I don't try to be something or someone I'm not. I appreciate how my life has turned out. Anyway, it's not as though I have any other choice. I guess that's what maturity means.

I enjoy my own company, but I also want to have fun with those who bring out the best in me. When spending time with friends, it's important to forget all the bad things that have happened in your life and just move on. I prefer to talk about fun things that have happened. Trust me, you'll be a much more popular guest at the party if you do. Now is the time to enjoy your happiness and share it with others.

This also means you should relish all you have and keep building upon it. Many of us who are retired are actually better off financially than we might initially have expected. This is what research shows, even though I will personally never belong to the new demographic on the market: *WHOPs (Wealthy, Healthy Older People)*. But it's all about prioritizing. We can no longer do everything.

Our needs change as well. Personally, I'm done shopping. My drawers and closets are full. I don't need any more stuff. I prefer the good old freebies, such as long walks and cross-country skiing in the wintertime, and swims and bicycle rides during the summers.

However, I often enjoy lunches out, as well as visiting the theater and going to the movies, all of which are a part of my active social life. All my expenses go to the service industry these days. I have enough *stuff*—so no shopping sprees for me!

4

DON'T DOWNSIZE

Being a happy old man demands space. So my advice to you is not to downsize your home as soon as you retire. You'll need a bigger space now, because now you can finally enjoy it. You don't have to rush through the house any longer. Relish that, at last, home is the only place you *have* to be. No more tunnel vision.

Take a look around you. With a little bit of luck, you'll have twenty more wonderful years in the home you spent a lifetime building.

5

NOW IS WHEN YOU NEED SPACE

When the children flew from the nest, they left big empty spaces, which you can now take full advantage of. You can create a workspace, a separate computer room, a music room, hobby hole, a workshop, or even a liberating junk room where you can do whatever you want and not have to worry about cleaning up before your guests arrive. Because you should have plenty of guests. After all, you now have the time to socialize!

So build a fire in the grate, pour yourself a drink, and play some of your favorite music. Enjoy all the good things that life has to offer now that you're finally, wonderfully free.

6

DON'T MOVE SOUTH

Many people debate whether or not to move to their summer home or to a warmer climate. It's not a bad idea—if many of your friends are there and if it offers you the chance to do all those things you've always dreamed of.

But as you get older, it's important to be familiar with and established in the place that you live. Life will be much more fun that way. By making use of the social circle you already have, you can extend your group of acquaintances without having to start from scratch. It's also good to keep in mind that you can still change your surroundings every once in a while by popping off on a trip or, if you're lucky enough to have one, to your summer home. It's good to change things up sometimes.

Even when you no longer work, summer is a special time of year—so prolong that summer feeling. Go to your summer getaway earlier in the spring and return later in fall; that way, you can actually create two different lives, with two separate networks and focuses. I love dozing off to the heavy buzz of bumblebees under the apple tree each September. Every lingering summer's day feels like a gift.

7

DON'T GET A DOG

As a kid, I always dreamed of having a pet dog. But now I've reached the conclusion that I shouldn't get one—at least, not until I'm really old and lonely. Don't get me wrong, if owning a dog is your hobby or big dream, this might be a good time to get one. But you should take into consideration how much time and responsibility a dog requires. It's like caring for a small child who never grows up. What's more, there aren't many places that will allow you to bring a dog with you. Many beaches have strict rules against dogs during the summer months. Not to mention the challenges of traveling with a dog. And all the shit you have to keep picking up!

8

DON'T BECOME A MICROMANAGEMENT GURU

Don't dwell on the small things. Expand your perspective and try to see the bigger picture. Most of us have hoarded too many old papers and odds and ends that should never have been saved in the first place—especially from the office. If you don't plan on writing your memoir, you should just throw out all these papers right now. Don't try to organize things that aren't worth organizing. I know you know what I'm talking about!

Throw away all the things that never gave you pleasure. If you're worried about what to throw out, ask yourself this question:

Will this matter to me in two years?

It rarely does.

9

BUT SAVE OLD
JOURNALS

Life is long. We've experienced so many amazing things that it's easy to forget some of them. But most things are still there, somewhere in the hard drives of our mind—we just need the password. I've kept a journal since I was eleven years old. If I pick up my journal from 1955, for example, and open to a random page (why not Saturday, October 29?) it reads like this:

"Timmy came by and we assembled my electric train. We built a long track that went all the way from the living room to the hallway. We kept driving trains back and forth and it was so much fun. After that, we went home to Timmy's. We were there for an hour and had a pillow fight. After that, I went home and went to bed."

Nothing more, nothing fancy.

But suddenly, that day opens up in my mind. I see it all: our home in Cleveland Park in Washington DC; the Maret School I attended; my play date with my classmate Timmy from England; his family's old Packard and their funny way of speaking English, a language I was just struggling to learn; how he didn't like the Swedish meatballs my mother made for lunch; and just how much fun we had all the same.

"Open Sesame!" This short little paragraph in my journal was all it took to remember. To think that so many memories came flooding back as a result of a few simple sentences in an old journal.

Memories are what we have left once time has come to an end. Without our memories, we lose both a sense of time and identity, and we lose our grip on the foundations we've built throughout our lives.

10

CERTAIN BOOKS
ARE INVALUABLE

If you've highlighted things in the books you've read, it's easy to find the password to your hard drive.

My high school geography teacher insisted that we highlight only the most important passages in the text; then we were told to study just the highlighted parts for our exams. I have continued to highlight in the books I read throughout my entire life.

Today, when I open one of these books, both the plot and the reasoning come back to me in just a few minutes—no matter what the subject matter is. Highlighting is a good enough password for me.

Such books are invaluable and should be cherished. It's important to hold onto the passwords to our memory banks for as long as we can. Once they're lost, they can never be retrieved.

Most of us have great memories. We don't forget as easily as we might think we do. That is something that makes this old man happy.

11

LIVE IN
THE PRESENT

Don't make things difficult for yourself. Live in the present—don't fight against the times. Everything didn't used to be better. You don't have to love the changes happening all around you (as we rarely do when we get older) but don't let them get stuck in the back of your throat like a fish bone. Because if you do, who will suffer? You.

12

LET GO OF FORMER PRESTIGE

It is my experience that men have a more difficult time letting go of their former prestige than women do. Too many of us have identified too heavily with our career personas. Just think of how important titles were for social status in the olden days. It was often even more important than the nature of the work itself. But a man who retires as an "accountant" and is replaced by someone who is called a "comptroller" will probably still have a negative reaction to it today. These two titles really do sound like they're from two separate worlds.

We've all been a little arrogant at one time or another during our lives. It's time to burst that bubble and open up to the world around us. Now we can talk to each other like we never have before. The hierarchies are gone, how liberating! This offers up many exciting new opportunities.

A person who is too caught up with prestige will actually limit himself socially; he will grow isolated. People like that are difficult to deal with and they often end up alone.

13

RESOLVE YOUR FEELINGS OF GUILT AND BITTERNESS

Many people spend their whole lives feeling guilty. Others carry a heavy bitterness inside. Often the reasons for these emotions are trivial, and in many cases, they begin with a misunderstanding. Sadly, it's often the case that nothing can be done about it, because some of the people involved have died.

But this is a very important health issue. Feelings of guilt and bitterness wear on a person's life force. It's like driving a car with the parking brake on. You end up with higher blood pressure and an increased pulse, according to medical studies. To quote a doctor's assessment, it can be "just as dangerous as smoking."

This is why it's time to come to terms with your feelings of bitterness or your guilty conscience. The key is to forget and move on; this is crucial to becoming a happy old man.

If some self-appointed agent of morality—and there are plenty of them out there—criticizes you for this, just turn it around on them and quote Jesus from the Sermon on the Mount: "Can any one of you by worrying add a single hour to your life? [. . .] Therefore do not worry about tomorrow, for tomorrow will worry about itself. Each day has enough trouble of its own."

That usually shuts them up.

Projects

14

NOW IS THE TIME TO DO ALL THOSE THINGS YOU'VE DREAMED OF

This is the time when you should think about what you really want to do, and what you've always dreamed of doing because now you have the time to do it. This is the time to focus on the possibilities, not the challenges. Having projects to focus on creates unity and meaning in your life.

If you want to travel, go ahead! Personally, I've already done most of my traveling after so many years living abroad. Now, my focus is on writing my books, spending time with my family and friends, and getting in a round of golf on those beautiful early-summer days.

Some people might find it stressful to start new projects now that we're finally free. There might be something to this, but don't forget that golden rule you learned during your professional life: the more you do, the more you have time to do. Try not to reduce your capacity too soon. Because how much fun is that? Besides, merciless Time will do it to us all soon enough.

15

DON'T BECOME
A DOGMATIST

Many older men who have no projects to focus on quickly become dogmatists who complain about everything and everyone. They look for opportunities to correct others as a way to simply make contact. They often seem to represent the "Official Point of View" or the "Silent Majority." You know what I'm talking about. I think we've all met that quiet older gentleman who bumps into us on purpose on the sidewalk just so he can say, "In this country we walk on the right-hand side."

That's just plain sad.

16

DON'T SPEAK IN THE CONDITIONAL TENSE

Don't talk about things you could have done but didn't, should have done but didn't, or wanted to do but couldn't. The conditional tense is the most dangerous of all (which our generation should still remember from grammar lessons!). It represents all that you could have done if circumstances had been different. The conditional tense doesn't lead to anything positive.

Other countries and cultures are more aware of their use of language. The first thing French psychologists do is to correct a patient's use of verb form; most often they're using the conditional or subjunctive tenses.

So make sure you speak in the present and future tenses about what you're doing now and what you're planning to do later on. And forget all the things you didn't do.

Enjoy the present. This is the moment that counts.

17

DON'T DEFEND YOUR PAST TO ALL ENDS

You're your own person now. You don't have to defend your earlier life, your former employers, or their products and services. I am no longer a diplomat. I am a free human being. It's not my concern what the Department of State does during world crises. So don't get offended when people speak badly about your former employer. His problems are not your problems anymore.

18

TELL YOUR
LIFE STORY

Everyone can do this. You don't need a
publisher or a readership. You have your family,
and that's enough. Children and grandchildren
will want to learn more about your life, your
parents, and your childhood. The happy times,
and the sad. But they often forget to ask before
it's too late, before you've forgotten it all, are
too tired, or are simply no longer here to tell
your story.

With today's new print-on-demand technology, it's easy to print your memories in book form,
even if you only want ten, thirty, or fifty copies.
It might cost you a couple hundred dollars, but it
will be a real, physical book that will sit on your

children's and grandchildren's bookshelves for many years to come. It's a great present and a comforting memory for them—and you!

19

GROW
YOUR
GARDEN

"If you have a garden and a library, you have everything you need," Cicero famously said. I would like to add that both are necessary for the soul.

Even as a young child, I had a small plot of land in our flowerbed where I could grow my own flowers. I bought bags of seeds, which I sowed, watered, and weeded. In the mornings, I went out to see what had happened during the night. I was just as delighted each time another flower had bloomed as I was the first time.

Today, people who are over-stressed and burnt out are advised to take up gardening because it's so therapeutic. As older people, we need to be connected to nature in order to find peace and happiness. A window box, balcony planter, or a flowerbed can be all you need, or join the conservancy of your favorite park. It's just important that you are able to grow something and follow its developments. Sit there and simply daydream for fifteen minutes every day. It will do wonders for your soul.

I now have a small flower garden of roughly five hundred square feet, and I watch it throughout the seasons. I asked a landscaper to help me build it, and it took us only three days to create this little gem.

Here, I have about thirty roses, two lilacs, a boxwood, a large hydrangea, a butterfly bush, a rugosa rose, and plenty of wild hollyhocks. I'm glad that I don't have grass in this little garden; this way, it keeps the weeds out and gives me peace of mind.

In my garden, I also have designed three small places to sit, two that sit one person and one for two people, which can be reached by small cobblestone walkways. In these nooks I've placed two large stones polished by the sea and a stone table, which has been shaped by nature itself.

All of this cost me about as much as I would have paid for a Caribbean cruise. The difference is that this little flowerbed will bring me happiness for the rest of my life.

Every morning I wander around my garden with my shears in hand, pruning the roses and picking a bouquet or two of flowers. This is where I read, invite a friend for tea or a drink, or perhaps take an afternoon nap.

20

STOP
TAKING
PHOTOS

I have spent my whole life taking photos. I've crafted some great albums for the family—not only with photographs but also with maps, newspaper clippings, and the children's drawings.

But enough of that. I no longer want to experience my surroundings through a camera lens. I want to be fully present in every moment. I don't feel the need to document everything anymore. When I travel these days, the camera stays at home. It's a great relief. Now, the children can take the photos and make the albums. It is their turn to document Grandma and Grandpa.

21

EMBRACE
FATE

I knew I wanted to write. That I ended up writing books for children and young adults was pure coincidence. Had you asked me when I was younger, I would never have guessed this would be what I would write. It was pure chance. But it goes to show that you have to let fate play a role in your life, and you have to grab opportunity when it presents itself.

22

DON'T BET ON THE IMPOSSIBLE

Here's a personal example of something I always wanted to do but never made provision for: playing music. My mother was passionate about jazz, and we shared that love. I've always lamented the fact that I don't play an instrument, but I always imagined I would learn to do so later in life.

It didn't turn out that way. I listened to jazz albums, and eventually it turned into background music. I made no real effort to learn how to play, and suddenly there I was, with free time on my hands.

But by then it was too late. If I had learned the basics before retirement, perhaps I could have built on that foundation. But at the age of sixty-five, I couldn't start something from scratch that requires such intense concentration and nimbleness. Playing an instrument is more demanding than I had allowed for.

Yes, of course, it's no one's fault but mine. I simply wasn't motivated or musically inclined enough. So the best thing for me to do was to move on. But I can still enjoy listening to my albums! Thanks to rock 'n' roll, our generation will never be truly old. Besides, I still hope to visit Nashville one day.

23

STOP ACTING TOO RATIONALLY

Not everything needs to be planned out. So if it sounds like fun, go for it—even if it's spontaneous. All my big decisions in life have been emotionally determined. That goes for both my family and my home.

I've always dreamed of owning a sports car—a dream I share with many other men. One day while at my oldest daughter's house, I randomly met a mother of three who had a little red Triumph Spitfire she wanted to sell. She showed me her spiffy little car, and I was jumping up and down with excitement. Before I knew it, we were speeding down the highway at 100 mph on a test drive.

It seemed like such an obvious decision, so we drove back to finalize the deal.

But when we parked in the driveway, I couldn't get out of the low-positioned bucket seat. I was stuck behind the wheel with a stiff back and straight legs. Finally, I managed to climb out of the car—on all fours and flat onto the pavement.

Naturally the deal was off.

The years had passed me by. I had waited too long. But at least I had tried. That too is important.

24

GO FOR
THE FUN STUFF

But the dream of owning a classic car
wouldn't go away, so I did a Google search for
my childhood favorites, such as Studebakers,
Buicks, and Rovers. Suddenly up popped a wonderful advertisement for a Rover 75 from 1953. It
was exactly the same kind of car my parents had
when I was in elementary school.

I took the train to the station where the seller
was waiting for me. As soon as I sat behind the
wheel of the old Rover, I knew I had found the
right car for me: steering wheel on the right (RHD)
and leather interior with wood panels.

The car oozed of Old England and a combi-
nation of smells from my childhood. It was like

stepping into a time machine. I became a child once again.

The old Rover was in excellent condition and although I could see some flaws, I didn't let them stop me. It was now or never. This was exactly what I had dreamed of for so many years in the United States, when I had subscribed to *Hemmings Motor News*.

When I asked my wife what she thought, she said sweetly, "Yes, you go right ahead."

I was actually quite surprised.

When I later asked how she could agree to this rather foolish expenditure without any argument, she explained, "I could see how happy it made you."

And I've never regretted that decision. Every time I take the Rover out, it's just as much fun as it was the first time. Everyone I meet greets me with a smile. That's reason enough to have it.

25

LET COINCIDENCE LEAD THE WAY

I chose writing. How did it begin? Well, just like most things in life, it was the result of pure chance. When I worked in New York, my daughters went to an all-girls school. In elementary school, they had a "Famous Women's Day," for which the girls portrayed different prestigious women throughout history. The school had a list of names they could choose from, mostly American, but there were a few European. But I immediately noticed that there were no Swedish women featured.

I took it upon myself to contact the Principal who, in American fashion, immediately welcomed me to the school and invited me to talk to the students about a famous Swedish woman. I chose Queen Christina, because she was only six years old when she became queen. She was someone the little girls could easily relate to. After the lecture, I said that I hoped that the school would include Queen Christina on their list of heroes from now on.

"Ah, but there's a problem," the Principal said. "The girls would need a book to consult."

And that's when she turned to me and said, "You write it!"

I instantly replied, "I'll do it!"

26

DON'T GIVE UP!

Over the next three years, I read everything there was to read about Queen Christina and I wrote every day. I was filled with the pure exuberance of writing, but when I showed the manuscript to my daughters, the youngest one said, "Dad, this is so boring no child will ever read it!"

For a second, I considered just giving up. But instead, I quickly recovered and said, "Take this red pen." I told my daughters to: "Cross out, underline, and add whatever you think is needed."

Quite frankly, I didn't want to let go of my writing project. I felt strongly that it would bring me a lot of joy later on in life.

When I got my manuscript back, it was covered with red marks, but I didn't despair—I edited and edited and edited some more. When the book was finally published, it was actually quite successful. And I was over the moon!

That's how I became the diplomat-cum-story-teller. My impulsive decision turned out to be a lucky draw.

27

YOUR INTERESTS CAN MAKE YOU MONEY

At this point, I've written twelve historical books for young readers. It adds that silver lining to my life, and the profits cover expenses, such as repairs to my Rover.

More and more retired people start their own companies in order to lessen their expenses. At this point, 25 percent of retired people's income comes from side jobs like mine. It's a new trend that may change the future of the workforce. More and more elderly people will end up working with fun, new things that also generate income.

An example:

My grandfather lived his life as a poor military officer. But he was a multitasker and aspiring inventor who registered several patents in the hopes of finding a more fun and profitable way to spend his time. But it wasn't until he started importing Twining's Tea from London that everything finally fell into place for him.

He quickly became so fascinated by tea that he started his own brand, and he traveled around the coffee-enamored country of Sweden to promote the benefits of tea drinking.

Wherever he appeared, the local papers called him the "Tea Major."

His sales increased with each year that passed. His biggest success was between the ages of sixty-five and seventy-five, when he sold twenty-two of his brand's different blends and became an official purveyor to the Swedish royal court. The day he sold his company, he was paid handsomely for it. A few weeks after his seventy-fifth birthday, he signed the contract and put his money in the bank. On his way home from the bank, he collapsed on the ground from a massive heart attack and died on the spot.

He was a happy man throughout his whole retirement, and he died happy. He became my role model early on.

28

LEARN TO
ENJOY YOUR
OWN COMPANY

Because of my writing, I have plenty of exciting things to do these days. I rarely have time to just sit on the couch; instead, I look forward to my time in front of the computer. But in order to be able to do that, you have to learn to enjoy being by yourself. This is an important lesson to learn for the future. Believe me, we'll just keep finding ourselves more and more alone with age.

These days when I read, it often ends up being research for my next book project. The great thing about this is that I remember what I have read, just like during my years as a student.

It's important to have a purpose to your reading—even if it's only to write an article in the local newspaper or so you can participate in a book club. At our age, it's good for brain health.

Unfortunately, reading for pleasure usually results in naps on the couch—only to wake up once the book falls onto the floor. Using our brains is vital.

Use it or lose it, as they say.

29

TAKE A
COLLEGE COURSE

Personally, I was always bothered by the fact that I knew so little about the ancient world, such as life in Athens and Rome.

It was in ancient times that the foundation was set for western society—the European as well as the American, even though fewer and fewer people realize it. Finally, this educational field trip of mine was going to happen.

I registered for the Culture and Society in Ancient Times course at Stockholm University. Sure, I had read on my own before but now it finally felt real, as I was held accountable for learning the subject and I had qualified academic professors to discuss it with.

I had planned to go to the lectures and read the textbooks but had no intention of taking the exams. But after a while, I was so absorbed by the subject and felt so challenged by it that I decided to take the exams after all.

After a little while longer, my competitive streak took over, and I wanted to earn decent grades so I wouldn't feel embarrassed in front of my young classmates.

I'm a very dedicated student now, and I'm having so much fun. But I don't take classes throughout the full school year, because that would get to be too much. I study during the spring semester, and my preference is to take part-time courses. Because, don't forget, you're doing this for fun.

30

TRAVEL IS MORE FUN
IF YOU MAKE IT
A PROJECT

When I travel today, I go to places I need
to learn about for my writing. This means I can
walk around Rome for hours, imagining what
it was like for the senators to walk through the
Forum Romanum before starting their debates at
the Roman Curia. It's exciting to see how things
start coming together, and I often feel like I'm
experiencing moments of epiphany. This fall, I'm
headed to Pompeii and Herculaneum!

31

FOCUS ON
HISTORY

If you don't have a favorite subject, I recommend studying history of some sort. There are many different historical subjects to choose from at the University. Check out the offerings at your local community college, many of which offer summer courses as well.

As an older student, I've noticed that I have an aptitude for historical subjects that cover vast periods of time and demand a broader perspective. This is our edge as "mature" students!

32

TALK TO YOUNG PEOPLE

Having discussions with young students
is a challenge. You learn a lot, and they enjoy
hearing about your experiences—so long as you
don't always insist on speaking first. Having lunch
at the University, surrounded by students and
textbooks, is a great way to prevent unnecessary
aging.

Discussing a common subject with younger
people is good for you. They have completely
different perspectives and interests you might not
have considered.

But we do have something in common: As
older people, we have lived a long time. Young
people want to live for a long time too. How can

you do that in the best way possible?

This is why we who are older have a responsibility to show aging from its best angle.

It's also why we can't whine in front of young people:

they run away immediately.

Just in case you didn't know.

Once again I will quote the wise Cicero:

"As I approve of a youth that has something of the old man in him, so I am no less pleased with an old man that has something of the youth. He that follows this rule may be old in body, but can never be so in mind."

In other words: There is still hope.

33

LET ONE THING LEAD TO ANOTHER

At the time of this writing, I've taken three advanced courses in addition to my first survey course on antiquity. One thing led to another without too much planning on my part. I've had an amazing time and have learned a lot. The ancient cultures have come to life for me and I've gained many new perspectives. It might even lead to the writing of a new book. Simply put, this happy old man has a new interest and a new project.

34

ALWAYS HAVE
A NEW PROJECT
IN THE WORKS

Make sure to always have a new project to start at the beginning of each season. The brain needs exercise just as much as the body does, and it's worth repeating: as long as you keep learning and growing, you do not age.

A good idea is to lay the foundation for your project with a symbolic gesture. When I begin writing a new book, I like to start at eight o'clock on New Year's morning. A whole year lies before me, and I feel rich in time and possibilities.

And perhaps I do feel a little self-righteous when I think of all the people still sleeping their restless sleep after a night of drunken New Year's celebrations, while I sit here awake and alert, enjoying my writing. But that, too, drives me.

35

DON'T LOSE TOUCH WITH THE TIMES

It's important to maintain contact with society unfolding around you. This is how you stay curious and keep yourself from becoming whiny.

I hold public office at the Building Committee in my local community. Here, I have the opportunity to meet people of all ages and from all different walks of life. This hopefully keeps me from limiting my perspective to my own age group and becoming unnecessarily conservative. You can't complain about the times without drawing yourself into the critique. You live now, accept that. It's much better to be a part of the times than to complain about how you are not. Because this is still *our* time—don't forget that. So go out and engage with your community!

36

DON'T BECOME A TECHNOPHOBE

Technical evolution is speeding up and permeating everything. That's why it's imperative that you don't isolate yourself from it. But, of course, you should choose to keep up to date with the technology you personally enjoy. You can't keep up with *all* the advancements.

I love word processing, email, and the Google search engine. Naturally, I order books and travel online. I love to Skype with my children in New York, so we can video chat without any costs whatsoever. And if you're tired of always being available, there's an app for curbing the clutter: MacFreedom. But other than that, I'm still my best freedom app. ☺

However, I still don't feel the need for Facebook. I have enough acquaintances with whom I don't spend enough time. Nor do I need to read my children's status updates. I am their father, not their buddy.

37

ACCEPT ASSOCIATION AND BOARD POSITIONS

It's fun and meaningful to give advice, especially as it's during your sixties and seventies that you've absorbed the most knowledge and can offer the best suggestions. Plus, now you can at long last see the bigger picture without being skewed by shortsighted, personal career interests.

In Sweden, we're not very good at utilizing this knowledge. It's different in the United States, where older people's experiences and efforts are valued. That's why they tend to serve as integral parts of company boards and community programs well into their eighties. They are expected to share their networks with the younger generations, which young people are truly grateful for.

And that's not to mention the great pleasure the elders get from helping.

But Sweden can change its attitude. We were the last EU country to adopt legislation against age discrimination. It was high time too, because for too long young and arrogant finance executives have created one bubble after the next, only for the market to crash repeatedly. Real estate, art, stocks, health-care companies—all have been speculated in over the past twenty years. The United States and Europe have sunk into a black hole of debt. Age and experience will surely be valued more highly in order to rebuild a more stable society. We're older, we're wiser, we're needed. We just need to prove how much we're worth.

38

DON'T LET THE NEWS DISJOINT YOUR DAY

The news on the radio and the TV can chop up our time. As newly retired people, we tend to watch the news several times during the day, as well as in the evening. However, most of us realize that it's largely the same news being delivered over and over again over the course of the day, often with the same interviews and the same voices. So just get off that couch.

I avoid the morning news programs because I have the newspaper to read instead, and I don't want shrill voices on the radio or TV to inflame my mood. It's rarely a good way to start the day.

I also avoid watching the news on the TV, since it's so easy for me to get stuck in front of it. The average Swede spends seven and a half *years* in front of the TV over the course of a lifetime. And the number is significantly higher in the United States—up to two months a year in front of the TV but then again, Americans often use TV as a background while doing other tasks. Still, that's important to be aware of now when there's so little time left.

In my opinion, the best thing about the radio is that you can multitask while listening to it. After my hip replacement surgery, I did physical therapy during the news segment. Paying bills, bookkeeping, or performing other boring tasks can be a smart way to get things done while listening to interesting radio programs. I realize Americans use the TV in much the same way.

39

DON'T ALWAYS KEEP TRACK OF TIME

The best way to break the magic of a nice dinner, movie, theater performance, or concert is to check the time. I've spent far too much of my life wishing that a concert, opera, or theater performance would end so I could hurry on to the next thing.

"You have the clocks, we have the time," my friends in Kenya always used to tell me. It's a very insightful statement.

So stop checking what time it is, but be sure to remember the days of the week. Even a happy old man has to keep track of the week. If not, you're bound to become too eccentric for other people to keep up with—or you'll just get confused.

40

STAY IN SHAPE

The best way to stay in shape is to take advantage of opportunities for physical exercise in your everyday life. I have a car, but I often ride my bike to do minor shopping. When headed to a meeting, or out to lunch, I don't take the bus the whole way there. Remember that you have to exercise every day in order to stay in shape so stay away from that car. If you don't stay in shape, you can count on reaching old age ahead of your time.

A good option is to plan a nice stroll each time you intend to go somewhere. Then you can feel good knowing that you got your exercise in for the day, and you can enjoy a relaxing evening.

But you should also engage in focused physical exercise. Staff walking, speed walking with skiing poles—a very popular activity in Sweden—is good but those kinds of walks have to be faster than you might think. Preferably you should be sweating. Save the leisurely strolls for when you're really old.

Water aerobics are great because the water carries most of your body weight. This means it's gentle on your joints. Cross-country skiing is good. So is swimming. Golfing is great if you've had hip replacement surgery. But make sure you walk over to the next hole, rather than riding in the golf cart.

Don't forget all the rewards of staying active on those dark fall evenings when the wind is whipping and a long walk feels like the *last* thing you want to do.

The more you move, the better you'll sleep. And the closer you'll stay to your ideal body weight. You'll feel better, stave off double chins, and you won't doze off while reading your favorite books. And you'll look fresh and healthy—yes, just like a happy old man!

41

DON'T WAKE UP
YOUR STOMACH
FOR NO REASON

Keep your meals to a sturdy breakfast, a nice lunch with friends, and dinner with the family. We don't need any more nutrition than that. When you have too much time on your hands, it's easy to start grabbing a snack from the fridge and to get caught with one hand in the cookie jar. But it never really provides the satisfaction you're looking for; instead, you'll just feel uneasy. Everyone with fluctuating weight knows what I'm talking about. Never eat at night, because when you do, you wake up your body and the whole system is set in motion again just when it was ready to wind down.

However, it's too late to start dieting at this age. Your body has found its shape. If you diet, you'll only look gaunt and sickly. So leave those few extra pounds alone. But boys, remember that beer is really just floating bread. It's more filling than you think.

Enjoy What You Do

42

DON'T HESITATE TO QUIT

Man, he seems to be _rushing around a lot,_ you might be thinking. But remember that it's better to take on too much and taper off than it is to never try at all. If it's too much for you, don't hesitate to quit. Get rid of whatever doesn't live up to your expectations.

You can resign from the boardroom, drop courses, or stop reading that book that's not as interesting as it sounded. You can leave a play during intermission. Don't let decorum hold you back. You're the only one making the calls in your own life.

43

ONLY SCHEDULE ONE ENGAGEMENT PER DAY

Schedule no more than one engagement a day in conjunction with lunch or dinner. The rest of the day should be dedicated to family, friends, exercise, a hobby, or a nap, which in turn can lead to new ideas and initiatives.

Retirement is about finding your own rhythm. If you don't, you'll end up carrying too much stress or you'll find that your days simply vanish with nothing accomplished.

These days, it feels as though time moves at a perfect speed. Yes, my life goes at my own pace now. It's my first little step toward balance and perhaps wisdom, which I gratefully embrace.

When I was working, I always had to rush to get everything done. I was always thinking ahead and I often wished I were somewhere else. These days, my life is all about living in the moment and not sitting around thinking about other things. This is called "Mindfulness"—a very fashionable word these days, and courses on the subject cost big money.

44

ENJOY
WHAT
YOU DO

It's not what you do or what the end result is that's important. What's important is that you're fully present when you do something. Pleasure takes practice. And enjoyment depends a lot on your own attitude. It all depends on your way of thinking. At our age, this is definitely worth repeating.

The curse of our careers is that we usually stress out from one subject to the next, from meeting to meeting, and we never stop for even one second to contemplate or to experience what's happening.

As a free person, you can now—for the first time—enjoy what you do. And if you don't enjoy it, you should really stop right now and do something else. You, and only you, get to decide.

45

MAKE GOOD
USE OF YOUR
MORNINGS

I always wake up early in the morning now, even though I no longer have to. I eat breakfast in bed and read my morning paper, which always feels like a great luxury. Sometimes I think:

Okay, you really can't just lie here any longer.
Of course I can!

After my lengthy breakfast, I take a walk, go swimming, biking, or skiing to get the blood pumping and to get some fresh air.

After that, it's time to start writing.

Mornings are plenty busy!

46

DON'T FORGET
TO NAP

It's easy to feel sleepy in the afternoon and it's a good idea to give in and take a nap. It's not necessary to always be doing something. Sometimes it's nice just to *be*. It's a good insight, perhaps even wise!

An afternoon nap is also a good way to keep from dozing off in front of friends and family in the evening, which is something that can easily happen at our age.

It feels wonderful to just doze off on the couch or easy chair, but it's better to go to bed and crawl under a blanket, or to retire on a lazy chair in the garden. You should make yourself comfortable. The feel of a pillow with a cool pillowcase increases the pleasure of falling asleep outdoors tremendously. I also enjoy using the eye masks I've saved from my plane travels, which allow me to fall asleep anywhere.

As a free person, you don't have somewhere to rush off to, so I usually allow myself to slowly drift to the surface of consciousness and then sink down into sleep once more—several times—before actually getting up. It's truly an underrated pleasure, I assure you.

47

MAINTAIN YOUR GOOD HUMOR

Laughter adds years to your life, or so the saying goes. It's actually scientifically proven: laughter releases endorphins into the body and these make us feel good.

Never does this hold truer than later in life. There is also more to laugh at—and more that you now dare to laugh about—when you come to a certain age and can look at the world with new perspective.

It's not always easy to laugh on your own. But there are useful tools even for this. Make sure to have some good old comedies at home. I love the old Laurel & Hardy movies. It's impossible not to chuckle when they start their routine.

Dark comedy is a certain genre I have come to enjoy when facing down illness. Being able to joke about death helps me through difficult situations. Humor is an effective way of stepping out of yourself and sometimes you need that—especially when you're about to be squeezed into the tight cylinder of an MRI machine.

48

KEEP
HOPE ALIVE

It's said that hope is the last thing that we as humans give up on. Unfortunately, I meet many old men who seem to have already lost hope. This is probably due to loneliness. After all, human interaction creates desire and hope for the future.

But it's important to remember that we do still hold the key to our own future. It's up to us what we do with the rest of our lives. We can choose to break bad patterns or to create new and better ones. We can choose hope.

49

BE MORE LIKE
THE DANES

Swedes have always felt that the Danes have more fun than we do—and the Danes agree!

Several European studies show that the Danes actually top the list when it comes to joy of life. They laugh twice as much as we Swedes do. It must be the Aquavit, the beer, the smoking, and the Danishes, of course.

However, the Danes don't top the list of people who live longest. In this category, the Swedes surpass the Danes by several years.

The connection is clear and the choice is yours. But perhaps we could be just a little bit more like the Danes. We don't all have to live life like a somber Ingmar Bergman movie, do we?

50

OR MAYBE A LITTLE BIT MORE LIKE THE AMERICANS

In total, I've lived in the United States for ten years. I lived in New York and in Washington, DC. Even as a young child, it struck me how much more fun American men seemed to have than my father did. They dressed in brighter colors and everyone seemed to have a rec room or a hobby space where they did fun things. This inventive mentality is the driving force behind all the successes of Silicon Valley, for example.

This impression only increased as I grew older. My American relatives who are my age have garages filled with classic cars of all types and models. The other year, my cousin Arthur set off on a cross-country road trip in his old Franklin from 1932. He followed Old Route 66, and it became a journey through both time and space. The highlight of his trip was stopping in at the Franklin club in Colorado, where a number of Franklin owners had gathered for a leisurely weekend.

Concerned, I asked him, "How did you know that old car was going to last the whole trip?"

"Well," he replied, "that was the exciting part!"

We should all learn to be more playful. Don't fret about problems before they happen and when they do happen, take them with a grain of salt. In all honesty, we no longer have too many important appointments to keep.

Among Friends

51

CHERISH YOUR FRIENDS

Cherishing our friends is another privilege of age. Now we have time to renew and deepen our friendships with loved ones both old and new. We have time to be together.

But sadly it's always not as easy as it sounds. Everyone seems to be busy or pretends to be, and we can't always be the ones to reach out. Acting as though we have a fully booked social calendar seems to be the preference of newly retired people. We are deathly afraid of looking like we have nothing to do. Or perhaps this is our first line of defense? Being alone is taboo.

If you've neglected your friends due to work, it might take some serious effort on your part to reestablish those friendships. The same thing goes for having lived abroad for many years, as I have done. Your friends have simply found new companions, which can be difficult to accept. It takes time to breathe life back into an idled friendship. Make that extra effort and reach out today.

52

IT'S THROUGH OUR FRIENDS THAT WE GET TO KNOW OURSELVES

It's almost solely through long-lasting friendships that we learn of the human condition and get a better understanding of who we really are. Now is your opportunity to deepen your friendships and personal insight.

This is very important because the most common complaint among the dead—if we could ask them—would probably be that nobody ever understood them deep down. So take pleasure in the fact that there's still plenty of time and there are so many positive things left out there to experience in the company of good friends.

53

ESTABLISH A LUNCH CLUB

Try to establish a standing invitation for lunch or dinner with a circle of good friends for a few times a month. It will be a good investment for the future, since older men tend to have smaller networks than women do, meaning they'll spend more time alone in their older days.

When I was about to retire, I contacted my oldest friends from my college days and we decided to set up a lunch for the first and third Tuesdays of every month at the same restaurant. If people can make it, all they have to do is show up. If you can't, there's no need to cancel or give notice.

That first time, twelve of us showed up, and I took it upon myself to make the reservations. To set the tone, we named our group "The happy old men." The name alone makes it more fun when we get together. Here, I laugh my deepest belly laughs and the air is always bursting with endorphins.

It's also nice to be able to talk about those annoying little things that happen as you get older with a group of people who can relate. *Oh, so I'm not the only one who wakes up in the middle of the night with cramps in my calf? Well, that's a relief to hear.* These lunches just continue on at the appointed times without any of us having to reach out.

"The happy old men" know each other from their college days, which is also good for if and when our short-term memory starts to fail us. Deep down inside, we're all former twenty-year-olds with shared memories. That's why we always have something to talk and be happy about.

Sometimes, a couple of us go to a museum or a movie after lunch. I usually play a few afternoon games of backgammon with one of them. All of this has an incredible feeling of freedom from responsibility to it, which brings me back to that familiar childhood mantra:

"Can Dag come out and play?"

"Yes, of course he can!"

Life is best before 12 and after 65!

54

JOIN CLUBS
AND ASSOCIATIONS

Join one of the many clubs or associations out there. I'm a member of a men's-only club in town, which has become my second home. I lunch there with friends and read international newspapers and magazines, especially my old favorite the *New Yorker*.

Through Rotary, I also have a lunch booked every Wednesday. It's a different network, one that includes women. Here we have the opportunity to listen to and converse with speakers who are often still in the middle of their careers. But you should join these clubs before you retire, so that you will be the new, young member. They usually have enough retirees as it is.

55

DON'T VISIT
YOUR OLD
PLACE OF WORK

You should avoid visiting your old place of
employment. Your name is usually scraped off
your old office the day after you leave. Your
coworkers now have other managers and other
priorities. You're no longer a part of their
network.

Perhaps they're on their way to their Wednesday afternoon meeting, and there you suddenly
are, holding them back. They're in a hurry while
you have all the time in the world.

It won't turn out well for either one of you.

Do I socialize with old colleagues? Yes, but
only the ones that became my personal friends.
But not even they are close enough to be a part

of my lunch gathering. At work we each had our designated role. It's nice not to have to play these parts anymore. A while back, I hurried by my old workplace. Suddenly, I looked up at the building and experienced the same feeling I would get whenever I walked by my old school:

"Oh well, that's a place I used to go."

It gave me a great feeling of freedom.

56

NOT ALL
MY FRIENDS
ARE STILL HERE

Some of my close friends do not belong to the world of the living. They exist in literature, where they always remain equally alive. I often return to them and they give me new perspectives on life—and a little bit of comfort. You should try it too.

The Russian dramatist Anton Chekov has played an important role in my life. No matter where I travel, I always buy tickets to Chekov performances. It doesn't matter what language the play is being performed in; I know them all by heart. Chekov was one of the first to transform daily life into drama, and daily life is what we live every day.

"One way or another, we have to live our lives, no matter what happens to us," Masha says in *Three Sisters*.

Time passes and everyone ages. When I was a young man, I identified with the idealistic Konstantin in *The Seagull*—the young man who strives to portray the big ideas. During middle age, Uncle Vanja's desires resonated with my own. Right now, I feel closer to the unhurried Gayev in *The Cherry Orchard*—the liberal uncle who makes eccentric speeches about everything and takes life as it comes. He would definitely fit in with "the happy old men."

Soon, the only character left to identify with is the eighty-seven-year-old Firs in *The Cherry Orchard*. But I still have a long way to go before I'm there!

Standing Tall

57

DRESS UP!

One of the benefits of my scheduled lunches is that I'm forced to dress up when I go into town. The happy old men always arrive in suits and ties.

A tie, handkerchief, bow tie, or buttoned-up shirt has the added advantage of hiding the old "turkey neck." And because of this, we look brighter and happier when we meet.

There's nothing sadder than meeting an old colleague in town who is dressed in a pair of worn-out sweatpants. Sure, I do own a pair, but I only wear them when I'm at home, in the garden, in the woods, or while I'm out biking.

In ancient times, one's age was judged by how good you looked—not by years lived, which many people didn't even keep track of. We too need to spiff up our aging bodies with a little bit of elegance. Whenever you meet your friends and acquaintances, they'll see a happy and fresh old man who is enjoying life. There's something to be said for that.

We shouldn't lose our earlier life roles, because if we do, we'll end up sliding into the anonymous "pensioner" identity with countless other, graying types. The truth is that the rest of the world treats "old people" like lesser beings, so don't let yourself be pigeonholed.

It's also a good idea to avoid becoming a part of those big swarms of retirees who push everyone out of their way and take up all the space. Chances are that they'll be labeled as old jerks.

58

DRESS
IN COLORS

When I turned fifty, I went from standard business ties to bright and happy red bow ties. I got tired of looking at the same, boring person in the elevator mirror each morning. I worked on the forty-fifth floor of a New York City skyscraper, so I had plenty of time to reflect. The happy red bow tie made me smile at my mirror self, and it still makes me smile today.

What's more, so many people smile at my bow ties, and sometimes they even make a kind remark. Smiles are highly contagious. They brighten the day and nurture the soul. It's a tiny investment that pays out in endless dividends. Yes, ultimately this is pretty simple: if you smile, people will smile back at you! If you look happy and smile, you will walk taller—or at least I do. Smiling and walking tall are great steps toward becoming a happy old man.

Family

59

BE A HAPPY OLD FAMILY MAN

Unfortunately, it's not always as easy being a happy old man within the family. There are many pitfalls and old roles that should be questioned—which is something you should do before your wife and kids do it.

Keep in mind that your adult children don't want the same things you do, and perhaps even your wife doesn't either. You constantly have to keep building new ties by doing fun things as a family, and you have to be open to other family members' opinions. Be generous with your family, in every way.

Be careful with your wording. Expressions such as "these days" or "in my day" tend to distance you from your children. They'll simply turn a deaf ear to what you have to say. There's a big difference between accepting the past and living in it. What does "in my day" really mean anyway? This is your day too. It's your shared day.

60

DON'T WALLOW IN SELF-PITY

There's nothing more depressing than a man, a father, or a friend who wallows in self-pity. Of course we all experience situations where we deserve pity, but if that's the case, it's better to have other people pity you than for you to pity yourself.

We're all willing to help a crying child, but very few care to console a self-pitying old man. If you constantly complain, you'll find yourself very lonely indeed. And then there will be a real reason to feel sorry for you!

Keep in mind that self-pity is often rooted in the language we use. All it takes is one wrong word to start a spiral you'll surely regret. And it's difficult to earn back trust and sympathy once you've fallen down that hole, because you'll have lost the pride you need to be viewed with respect as a human being—not to mention as a happy old man.

61

ALWAYS KEEP A FEW MINI BOTTLES OF CHAMPAGNE IN THE FRIDGE

This is a really good piece of advice.
I always keep a few mini bottles of champagne chilling in the fridge to liven up the mood during smaller occasions. They are equally useful for those gray Monday afternoons when you and someone you care about have had a misunderstanding. Make sure to use mini bottles, because you'll probably question if it's worth opening a big one if there are only the two of you.

If you have something else on hand that's tasty, go for that too, but remember that champagne has a special symbolic and celebratory value.

62

DON'T DISCUSS PROBLEMS AT NIGHT

Another good idea is to avoid bringing up problems or trying to discuss difficult questions in the evening.

"Let's discuss this in the morning," I'll usually interrupt my wife by saying when she starts to bring up difficult topics. Problems are always easier to solve in the morning. This also keeps you from getting worked up and losing sleep over the matter.

But if you do postpone, you really need to be willing to engage in that serious conversation the following morning.

It won't work unless you do.

63

RETIRE AT THE
SAME TIME

Otherwise it might not be much fun at all. I retired two years before my wife, and for those two years, we lived in two separate worlds with two completely different points of view. This was very frustrating. In my wife's eyes, I did nothing all day long, which meant that the cleaning, washing, and cooking should fall to me.

But I was actually busy, because I was in the middle of building my new life of freedom. We basically had two different rhythms and two different networks. It was almost like living double lives.

64

IT'S DEFINITELY TOO LATE TO GET A DIVORCE

If you were considering divorce for some time, you should have filed when you were in your fifties. It's simply too late now. At 65+, you don't want to waste the emotional capital the two of you have built up over the years. Letting it end in divorce would be tragic for you both. The reasons are clear to everyone, not least to your children.

This is why it's important to plan your continued life together in such a way that you both have fun.

Not to mention your children would almost certainly distance themselves from you if you break up the family so late in the game. Then you risk ending up completely alone. And think of it: You would have to divide all your property, sell the things you share, like the apartment or the house and your summer home. You might not even be able to keep the photo albums.

It's during retirement that the power of a strong relationship becomes apparent. Like a pair of swans, you should approach the last portion of your lives together.

Until death do you part.

65

BUT IT'S DEFINITELY TIME TO MOVE IN WITH SOMEONE

If you're single and unhappy about being alone, it's definitely time for you to do something about it. Single older gentlemen still have their appeal because there are so many fewer of them than there are single older women.

Since it becomes more and more difficult to get to know new people as we age, perhaps it's time to reunite with that high school sweetheart who might now be a widow. You'll have plenty to catch up on, and you'll already have a great foundation to continue building upon—even if you should be prepared to compromise. After all, you've lived different lives up until now.

In a best-case scenario, it can be the beginning of something new.

That, or you might end up becoming really close friends, which isn't bad either!

66

SHIFT YOUR
PARENTING ROLE

Now that we're older, my children and I
have different roles. They're in the prime of their
lives and I'm watching from the sidelines. They
now hold the big responsibilities, while my authority has gradually diminished.

This is one of the reasons why we have to cultivate our own lives as we get older. An old and
bored parent can easily become a strain on their
grown child. This lessens our value in their eyes.
It's probably the worst thing that can happen to a
parent/child relationship. Children don't want to
feel like their parents are dependent on them.

A few years ago, I was hit with a few serious
reality checks, which ended with my daughters

sighing in unison, "Dad, you are completely hopeless!"

It forced me to reconsider my standing. What was I doing wrong? Was I still trying to set the ground rules? Was I pointing out things I considered important, but were no longer relevant to the younger generations? Was I trying to give them unsolicited advice in situations where the answer was obvious? Clearly it was something.

Take a look at your relationship with your children. How can you have the most fun and avoid the pitfalls? Often it's best to start doing completely new things together and, if possible, visit new places instead of the old. In our home (our daughters' childhood home) and at our summer home, the roles are usually set in stone, so it can be helpful to plan for visits on neutral ground.

Try not to walk into your child's home as if it were your own. Surprisingly, many parents open cabinets, pull out drawers, arrange flowers, and turn lights off and on as if they were in their own house. It can be very belittling, not least to your sons- and daughters-in-law. Behave like a guest— a pleasant, noncritical guest. Also, remember that you have different priorities. You are now your children's second choice when they consider how they would like to spend their Saturday or Sunday afternoon. This doesn't mean they love you any less; they just have different priorities and have things to take care of. Most likely, they are being steered by their own children just as much as they used to steer your time.

67

CONTEMPLATE YOUR NEW ROLE

The last couple of times I have been a guest at my children's homes, I've let them decide what we should do. I've let them take the reins completely. Rather than questioning them every step of the way, I just talk about fun things I do these days—not what I used to do back in the olden days.

This also pushes me to stay active and do fun things. It's not just about appearing happy, but actually striving to be so.

68

GET TO KNOW YOUR CHILDREN

Retirement is a golden opportunity to get to know your children as adults. It's important for them and for you that you cherish this time before it's too late. It saddens me to think that I never really got to know my father before he passed away, as he died very young. So don't hesitate to have real conversations with your children now that you have time to do so—if and when they feel like it, that is. There's a time and a place for everything, and it's up to you to find those moments.

However, it won't work if you keep sticking to the past. Your reality is no longer theirs; they may remember shared experiences differently.

The best thing to do is to realize that we all have flaws of one kind or another. Perhaps we can all find new common ground together. Nothing makes children happier than parents who are open-minded enough to see old issues from a new perspective. Go ahead and surprise them!

69

HELP YOUR CHILDREN WITH THE SMALL THINGS

When I hear that my children have a practical problem, I'll gladly offer to help. Young people who are working overtime and caring for their own children are hard-pressed for time. Fitting practicalities like getting their car serviced might prove impossible. So I'll offer to take their car in, and at the same time I create a little field trip for myself.

If my children need a ride to the airport, I'll happily drive them. They get there quickly, comfortably, and without breaking the bank paying for a car service, while I get an hour or so of pleasant conversation. This is what quality time is all about in old age.

Plus, this increases my chances of getting computer help the next time the children come to visit!

70

BUT STAY AWAY FROM THEIR BIG PROBLEMS

Don't get involved in your children's big life problems. They need to solve them on their own and there's very little we can do about that. Just remember that they're adults now and their lives are their own.

If you engage too much, it's easy to end up in conflict with them. You then risk losing your own balance, and you'll have many a sleepless night ahead of you. And then, all my advice to you will have been in vain!

71

REMEMBER THERE ARE OTHERS IN WORSE SITUATIONS

"One more step, you old bastard, and I'll kill you!" the young Jan Myrdal threatened his father, Nobel Prize winner Gunnar Myrdal, as he raised a chair above his head.

This was part of everyday life for the most famous Swedish family of the twentieth century, but luckily most of us don't endure such conditions.

But by studying the Myrdal family, we can learn that we all have the right to our own experiences— both parents and children. There are always two sides to one picture. It's worth considering this ahead of time, before our relationships with our children suffer. As parents, we've enjoyed many years of authority, so we are the ones who should take the first step to listen and understand before it's too late.

72

TREAT YOUR CHILDREN AS OFTEN AS YOU CAN

If things are stressful for the young family around dinnertime, this old man offers to pick up dinner from a nice restaurant instead. I pick up the tab because I know their income needs to cover a million other things. There's no better way for me to spend my money than on being generous with my children. And we're not talking big sums here, since we don't see each other every day.

The alternative is that they receive that same money as an inheritance once I'm gone, but then I won't be able to play a part in the spending of it—which is the fun part! It's better to give money with a warm hand than a cold one. And not to mention there's nothing more provoking than old people who just sit around and expect to be treated to everything when they're out with their children.

73

KNOW WHEN TO KEEP QUIET

Now to the most difficult part: keeping quiet at the right moment. Knowing this is true wisdom.

One example:

The children are driving me to the airport in New York, as I'm going back to Sweden after a weeklong visit. It's only a few miles to the airport but we're short on time, a fact that I've kept strictly to myself. My behavior has been exemplary.

That's when I realize that the gas tank gauge is pointing at red for empty, and I almost have to bite my tongue to keep from saying anything. Up front, they're chatting away happily, but all I can do is stare at the gas meter. We will soon reach the highway where there are no gas stations. It's becoming more and more difficult to keep quiet, but I manage. That's when they finally realize there's a problem. They start bickering about whose fault it is, but the most important thing is that they're not blaming me. I just gaze out the window and don't say a word. They turn off the highway to fill up at the nearest gas station and once again we're on our way. All is well. I exhale. When we say goodbye at the airport I get my reward:

"Dad, you're such an easygoing guest!" my daughter tells me.

"Next time, stay two weeks!" my son-in-law says.

What a way to make this old man happy.

74

PAY CLOSE ATTENTION TO YOUR OWN ACTIONS

Truth be told, I had to exert plenty of self-discipline that week. I was careful with what I said and what I did. It's a good idea to avoid saying things that can be construed as judgmental or condescending, and to avoid situations where you need to control your own enthusiasm.

It can be easy to relapse, since children live so differently than their parents. But it was a healthy exercise and I had to learn to take on the role of the nice father and father-in-law. And I had so much fun!

But then there are also so many bad habits that have to be broken. I guess that's what living an active life is all about—to constantly change and improve oneself. Even when kids are small, they're not easily influenced. I've really only managed to influence my daughters once.

Let me share this story (it will work equally well on grandchildren):

I realized that my children would never fall in love with literature or become "true readers" if I kept buying them books and talking about it all the time. I would smother them with my enthusiasm and we all know what that does! Instead, I bought the whole series of Dover Thrift Edition classics, which at the time only cost a dollar apiece. I hid the box with all 125 books, and every once in a while I would scatter a few of them about the house without so much as a word. The girls picked up some of them and read them, while others they left untouched.

I realized that I had succeeded when my youngest daughter wrote an essay for school about the British poet William Blake. She got plenty of praise from her teachers and she was especially proud that she had found the book herself.

Wisely, I didn't say anything.

The results extended beyond my wildest dreams many times over. It wasn't until three years later that I was found out, but by that time my success was already cemented. One of my daughters became a literary scout in New York and the other became a literary agent in Stockholm!

75

YOU DON'T HAVE TO LISTEN TO EVERYTHING

This reminds me of a conversation I over-heard in my childhood. As my grandmother and my mother were chatting, my grandmother would occasionally address something to my grand-father, who was reading a newspaper in his armchair. He didn't reply.

"Is he having a hard time hearing these days?" my mother asked.

"Oh no," my grandmother replied. "He only listens when he wants to!"

Very wise!

76

YOU DON'T HAVE TO COMMENT ON EVERYTHING

The best way to avoid conflicts with your wife, children, friends, other drivers, strangers on buses, trains, and airplanes is to keep certain things to yourself. We're born to live life, not to keep a running commentary on it. You'll save energy and feel more at peace if you keep silent on some things.

During a trip to Russia, I stopped to visit the monks at Valaam Monastery on Lake Ladoga. It was against the rules to speak during mealtimes. In the beginning, one comment after another popped up in my head, but I never said them out loud. At first, it felt strange, but after a while, a sense of peace came over me.

It can be very peaceful to stop the automatic flow of impulses. It's really healthy to just be quiet once in a while. Try it sometime, but give your family forewarning. Otherwise they might think there's something wrong!

77

GIVE YOUR GROWN CHILDREN SOME PRIVACY WHEN VACATIONING TOGETHER

When your adult children come to visit at the summer home, it's important to be smart about it. According to studies, half of all families with several generations vacationing together under the same roof end up quarreling.

The most obvious reason is that we fall back into our old roles as parents and children. The second reason is that the space is usually pretty cramped, and because of this, we start driving each other crazy pretty quickly—especially if the weather isn't cooperating and everyone's irritated because of it. The parents rule and admonish while their grown children bicker and disagree. It's never a good situation. We're also talking about several days—if not weeks—together, in a small house that tends not to be the most comfortable to begin with. The mood can easily become tense, and then you might find it difficult to remain a happy old man. So it might be smart to find creative ways to avoid this.

My family has decided on the following:

When our children with their own families come to visit, we spend a few days together at the beginning, and then my wife and I go visit friends for a time, to return at the very end of our children's vacation. This allows us to try new things that we never did while we were working and had limited vacation time.

At the same time, the young families get some time alone to discover all the fun things to do in the area. They also get a chance to learn how to take care of the house, which is good, since one day they will probably take it over.

78

BEING WITH YOUR GRANDCHILDREN SHOULD ALWAYS BE ENJOYABLE

Spending time around young children can be rejuvenating. It gives the older generation a chance to experience the pure magic of a young child's vivid imagination. But you can only do this for certain amounts of time, and you have to set your own limits.

Of course, you should be of help when it comes to babysitting the grandkids. A day, an evening, or a sleepover is something I truly enjoy, but anything more than that leaves me feeling exhausted. I especially can't do several days in a row, unless I'm in the right frame of mind.

During the summer, it's great fun to spend time with young children, but one week is usually my limit. The best thing to do is to get all the little cousins together without their parents, because children tend to be in the best of spirits when they're in new and unusual situations. In my family, the kids call it "Camp Grandma." It's a lot of fun when they arrive, but it's also nice when they leave, because unlike the super powers their parents have been gifted with, nature has not granted grandparents the same boundless energy.

79

WATCH OUT FOR SICK GRANDCHILDREN

Now that you're older you have to say no to being around the grandchildren when they're sick. According to our family doctor, the infections small children get can be almost deadly for us older folk. Following her advice has made her very unpopular among young parents in our neighborhood. But I do believe her. At our age, a sniffling child can easily leave us bedridden for several weeks. Research supports this. Doctors say that older people are ten times as likely to die from a seasonal flu than younger people.

Small children need to go through about thirty different cold viruses before their immune systems fully develop. How many can you handle?

80

DISCOVER
NEW FAMILY
MEMBERS

Most of us have lost touch with a few family members over the years, including cousins who used to be close to us yet now feel like complete strangers. How this happens usually has nothing to do with ourselves, but rather how our parents got along with their siblings (relationships which most of us don't have the privilege of understanding). Because of this, we also don't have any part in any finger pointing.

So don't hesitate to reach out to long lost relatives. It might end up being more fun than you imagine. You have so much in common to talk about: your childhoods and your grandparents. However, it's best not to talk too much about your parents' generation, because this is usually where the conflicts are buried.

There's no good reason to carry family feuds on into the next generation. The summer home your father lost to his brother is gone and will be forever. Your cousin who owns it now has nothing to do with the choices his parents made. It could probably be a lot of fun to revisit the old house now that you're all older and wiser. It can also give you new perspectives on your own family. There are certainly more sides to old family feuds than the ones you've heard from your parents.

81

AVOID FAMILY MEMBERS WHO CAN'T RESOLVE THEIR OWN ISSUES

Certain relatives neither can nor want to find solutions to their problems. They seem to revel in their problems by constantly dwelling on them. It's their big life project and their pastime. And they can never forget.

Sit as far from them as you can during family gatherings and don't fall into the trap of joining in these discussions. If you do end up conversing with them, just smile and talk about something neutral. Make it a game—one that you have to win—to never get irritated by their whining. I promise you that they'll get tired of it eventually. And in turn you might find completely new friends among your other relatives.

82

BE GENEROUS TO YOURSELF, BECAUSE THEN YOU'LL BE GENEROUS TO OTHERS

Many older people I've met skimp on every little thing they can. I've done it too, and I still do it. But remember that it's now or never to have fun with spouses, friends, children, and grandchildren.

I still end up cheating myself—both in big and small things. There's the expensive wine I saved for so long that it went bad, and the beautiful cashmere jacket that I've never even used, or that exotic trip that I'm still not sure I'm going to buy for the whole family. I regret doing this, but I can't help it.

I've also felt a certain pride—which I'm cashing in way ahead of time—in knowing that

I'll be able to provide my children with a decent inheritance. Perhaps this stems from the old days when we didn't have social security benefits. And who knows, perhaps those times will return soon.

Nevertheless, being generous with yourself and others now, while you are still alive to enjoy it, is just as important as planning for a future beyond your lifetime.

Be Generous to Yourself

To you

83

STOP BEING
SUSPICIOUS

You only feed your own worries. You don't have to lock the front door each time you go out to the garden or run an errand.

Those teenagers aren't interested in your beat-up old bike.

That suspicious looking stranger doesn't want your fourteen-year-old Volvo.

And I really don't think your waiter will try to overcharge you on the tab this time either.

84

DON'T GET
WORKED UP

I've stopped getting worked up over things that once used to bother me. This relates to both big things and small. It's not easy, but it all comes down to you making the decision not to let things bother you. It will give you an inner peace and a feeling of being pleasantly indulgent.

Just leave it alone, I now think stoically.

When I walk through streets and plazas, I don't care how other people walk. I go my way and they go theirs.

When I drive, I no longer get anxious over how other people drive. I don't let anyone disturb my peace of mind. I simply don't care about them, and I just focus on the general rhythm of the traffic.

85

DON'T WAGE WAR ON THE YOUNG

Sweden has a well-developed social security system. In the United States, such systems are all privatized. However, everyone contributes to Medicare and Social Security to some extent. The collective problem is that most systems are overburdened and underfinanced. And the economical system is not improving by the fact that we all live longer and the world population keeps growing. This is why the best thing to do is to avoid waging war against younger generations. It's a conflict we are bound to lose.

It's important for all of us who are older that as many people as possible are working and paying taxes. The more people who work, the healthier the social security system is for us, because it's the younger generation who are paying for this—just as we once did for our parents.

That's why we should agree on all things that make it more profitable for our children and their generation to be productive citizens. This isn't politics. It's common sense for all generations when they reach retirement age.

86

AVOID PEOPLE WHO DRAG YOU DOWN

Now that you're free, you no longer have to have the tactical considerations that once forced you into silence or into agreeing with people you don't like.

Many people begrudge other people's successes and are jealous.

Not everyone wants what's best for you.

Now you can finally break free from them and their negative influence. The best thing to do is to just forget about them and move on. Don't let them sink your high spirits.

Trying to settle the score will only mean meeting them on their side of the court, which is a place you should avoid at all costs. Besides, it's usually a waste of time.

You can also turn this around. Jealousy is actually the loser's way of celebrating the victor. Deep down, bitter people are often just jealous of your successes, many of which you yourself have forgotten or taken for granted. So this really is something to be happy about.

This insight should also make you never want to be jealous of anyone ever again. Be happy that your friends and family are doing well. You'll benefit from their success by receiving more invitations, meeting new and exciting guests, having happier conversations, and enjoying better wines. Your friends' successes are also your own.

87

STOP
CHASING
WEEDS

This is important advice for those of you who have a garden. At our age, we should keep weeding duties to a minimum. It's a fight that most of us have already lost, anyway. These days, I look at the dandelions with indifference. It's a huge relief.

And stop chasing the figurative weeds as well. It's time to stop bickering about things that will always remain the same and that really don't make a difference anyway. You know exactly what I'm talking about.

88

STAY AWAY FROM THESE TOPICS

There are conflicts in the world that will never be resolved because both parties are both right and wrong at the same time, and because they have so much hate for each another. One such topic is the conflict in the Middle East. Steer clear of this topic and don't even discuss it with your children. There's no better way to ruin a social gathering. Trust me, I worked in the Swedish State Department, so I should know.

Religion has also become a tainted topic of discussion these days, but I have a good first line of defense. If someone suddenly starts talking to you about religion and it's too late to simply pull away, surprise them with the following statement:

"Isn't it amazing how smart the ancient Romans were? They always offered to let a stranger put his god inside the Roman temples so that god also could be praised. They figured you never knew when that new god might prove helpful." The ancient Greeks were even more ingenious. In Athens, there was an altar with the inscription:

"In honor of an unknown god."

They simply couldn't be sure that they had encountered all the gods yet. So let's be as wise as the people of ancient times. These are some of the valuable lessons I have learned at the university in my old age.

89

GIVE UP THE TIRESOME ATTEMPTS TO CLEAR OUT YOUR DESK

The reason is quite simple. If you haven't gotten your desk in order by now, you never will. It's just a waste of time and a burden.

Not everyone will have every aspect of their lives in order and perhaps you just happen to be one of these people. I am too. Accept it.

Certain issues only get resolved with time, which is something we should be thankful for. The trash can and the backspace button are great tools for those who use them. So throw away that box you labeled "Strings too short to use" once and for all!

90

STOP GOING TO AUCTIONS

Ten years ago my wife "forbade" me to go to antique auctions and similar events. It wasn't easy because I was always excited to find "treasures." But in reality, I was coming home with expensive items we had no space for.

The urge to buy meaningless things has subsided. I have attained peace of mind.

Now, I'm the one selling all my excess stuff at auction and I'm amazed at how many old people—many with one foot in the grave—prowl the floor, inspecting the goods. Yes, that's exactly what it looks like, so beware!

91

GIVE AWAY YOUR OLD THINGS

Most of us are still holding on to far too many objects and tchotchkes that we've inherited or purchased at some point during our long lives. Now is the time to give these items away to your children, grandchildren, or friends for Christmas or birthdays, rather than buying them computer games, avatars, or make-up and other things you don't understand anyway. You just end up getting the wrong things, and their gifts will get returned.

If you follow this advice, you won't have to push through crowded stores at Christmas time and you'll save a lot of money that can be spent on other fun things instead. Saving both money and trouble is quite a bargain!

This also makes it easier for your children when you're gone. There will be fewer things to take care of and sort through, since it's not like we can bring these things with us when we die. It's sensible advice to follow.

And, what's more, old items tend to be greatly appreciated by the recipients because most of what you own is now fashionable again or would be considered antique. If you're unsure, just slip a check inside that old vase. That way, you can't go wrong.

92

SELL YOUR OLD
STAMP COLLECTION

Almost everyone born in the '40s has various collections stored away in the attic. I kept my stamps and coins up there.

Nothing is more difficult to sell and value since both coin and stamp collecting is now almost obsolete.

I managed to sell the stamp collection for a couple hundred dollars, and I realized the coin collection had disappeared during one of our moves. They're just things and nothing I will lose sleep over. The important thing is that I no longer have to worry about them.

93

BUT SAVE THE THINGS THAT REALLY MATTER TO YOU

I have a few things that do mean a lot to me, because they bring back memories or smells from the past, just like the Madeleine cake did for Marcel Proust.

Usually, it's the most unexpected thing, without any real inherent value, that you cherish. A sugar bowl from my grandparents, an old Madeira glass from my college years, or the engraved Russian tea glasses from my time as a young attaché in Moscow. These are items that take me back, and I want to experience those memories again and again. Preserve and cherish these time capsules in your own life.

Some Practicalities

94

IF YOU LIVE IN A CITY, BUY MONTHLY PASSES FOR BUSES AND TRAINS

I used to buy single tickets for all buses, trains, and subways. This kept me from going into the city, or I'd find myself hiding behind the newspaper hoping the conductor wouldn't see me.

This meant that I limited my own mobility and developed petty habits that, in the long run, would have been highly unattractive and would have aged me ahead of my time. Luckily, I realized this before any serious damage was done.

95

USE YOUR MONTHLY PASS
TO DISCOVER
NEW WORLDS

These days, I always have a monthly pass and take the bus or commuter train whenever and wherever I want. My wife and I often take the train to an unknown station and walk our way back home. We get to see new places and don't have to look at the same old houses in the same old neighborhoods, which will sometimes lead to no walks at all.

When we get tired of the train, there are always plenty of buses to choose from. It's almost like having a diplomatic passport!

96

BECOME A TOURIST
IN YOUR OWN CITY

A friend of mine recently pulled me into a
project of his own: a journey to discover all the
districts of Stockholm—including the suburbs.
Equipped with our guidebooks, we'll start off
early in the morning and travel against traffic. In
the morning, we'll enjoy a cup of coffee and a
pastry at a café that looks like something straight
out of the '50s. Sometimes we'll start up a conversation with the owner and get to hear about the
life and times of Sweden back in the day.

Then we'll walk around various malls and
main streets. On a balcony in a new mall, we'll
have a big glass of wine in the middle of the
day—a special deal for retirees—and watch

young people as they roam around trying on the new fashions in the boutiques below. It's an exotic experience to watch who buys and who doesn't.

Later on, it's time for lunch at a classic bar and grill. Afterwards, we'll rest up with some newspapers and magazines at a local library. We end the day at another café with a cup of coffee and a pastry and then we head back home again.

When I put the key into the lock of my front door, it feels as though I have come back from traveling abroad. This urban exploration is something I plan to do the next time I go to New York for a longer period of time. There are so many neighborhoods and worlds to explore, and they're all just a metro card away!

97

TAKE ADVANTAGE OF
THE GOOD OLD FREEBIES

The lives our children and grandchildren live are becoming more and more expensive, since most modern entertainment costs money—a lot of money. I don't know if this makes them happier. It doesn't make me happier, but naturally I don't tell them that.

For those of us who are retired, there are so many opportunities to enjoy the good old freebies of nature. Walks of all kinds are a given, just like biking excursions and swimming. Morning swims always feel as glorious to me as walks on endless white-sand beaches.

During the winter, we go cross-country skiing almost every day. Gliding along the tracks is wonderful. There's no better exercise where you get to move all your muscles at a slow and steady pace. And taking a nice warm shower afterward feels like such complete luxury. After that, you can settle into the couch with a cup of tea, a good book, and a clean conscience.

This is why there is so much to look forward to about the winter. It's particularly important to stay a happy old man during these months. Whining about the cold, darkness, and snow is something we often do, but it doesn't make things better. It's just a waste of time. We don't live in the South Pacific. We live right here.

98

MAKE TRAVELING BY CAR A FUN EXPERIENCE

These days, when we travel by car we listen to audio books. It makes driving the six hours to our summer home easier to do at the legal speed limit. The trip passes by quicker and we have a great time. We also arrive feeling rested, since we haven't spent the trip tensing up and stressing out.

We've also started stopping along the way to visit friends, because we're really not in a hurry any longer. It's a nice way to reignite friendships.

We also take time out to stop and buy local delicacies. In New York, we get apples and corn, on Long Island we pick up wine and fruit pies, and in Vermont we buy apple cider and maple syrup. When traveling in Sweden, we make the obligatory stops for crayfish, wild strawberries, and fresh-baked bread. The list of specialties is getting longer and longer and our trips are becoming more and more fun. Also, when driving in America I always make a stop at the presidential home museums—the latest one being Calvin Coolidge's house in Plymouth Notch, Vermont. It takes a whole day, but since we're retired, time is no longer an issue.

99

AVOID THE
SIX DEADLY
SINS

If you've followed my advice thus far, you'll avoid the six classic deadly sins—jealousy, rage, gluttony, greed, lust, and pride—that have plagued mankind throughout history.

But isn't there a seventh deadly sin?

Yes, there is, and it's called sloth. But I have a hard time considering sloth a deadly sin for older, retired people. We no longer have to take responsibility for all the trouble in the world. At this age, we have the right to choose our engagements, to become more stoic and more observant.

"Do we always have to *do* something?" an old friend asked me. The answer is a resounding

"No!" The important thing is that you enjoy what you do—or what you don't do.

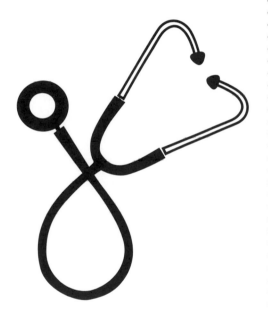

Sickness

100

IT'S ESPECIALLY IMPORTANT TO REMAIN A HAPPY OLD MAN WHEN YOU'RE SICK

Yeah, sure, it's easy to be happy-go-lucky when you're healthy, I can already hear you saying.

Actually, it's even more important to remain positive when you're sick, because that's when you need it the most. Positive thinking has proven to be the best medicine.

I know what I'm talking about, because I have had cancer as well as heart problems, and most recently, I went through hip replacement surgery. Good fortune comes and goes, so it's imperative that we keep a positive outlook during our low points. It takes some serious effort, since both cancer and heart problems are essentially an attack on our life force. But in the end what matters is not your situation, but how you handle it.

When I had cancer over ten years ago, I was forced to take an inventory of my life, and that's when I realized I wanted to live my life to the fullest. To simply enjoy it, to stop complaining, and to become a happy old man. It's better to be ready for anything rather than trying to guard yourself against everything—you'll fail no matter what. Life happens. Live in harmony with your destiny instead of fighting against it, and do your best to be happy nonetheless.

So it's a good idea to stay away from programs or people who sensationalize illness and try to scare us. Newspapers are especially prone to doing this.

This is what the day's headlines were when I wrote this chapter: "Lack of sleep can cause dementia" and "A regular migraine can actually be a stroke."

This is how the simplest reasons for a bad night's sleep become imagined diseases, and many people end up fretting for no reason at all. We've all had a sleepless night or two or experienced that intense headache.

It's the beginning of a downward spiral of worries, doctor visits, and endless Web MD searches. Stop before it's too late and before your health turns into your full-time job. The fear will keep you from enjoying life while you're still able to. I'm also convinced that worrying about being sick can actually make us sick.

101

THIS IS WHAT YOU SHOULD DO WHEN YOU GET SICK

When I had cancer, I underwent radiation therapy for a whole spring. My fellow patients didn't look too happy. As we all know, a third of all cancer patients end up dying.

Because of this, I made a point of playing squash or skiing before I went in for my radiation sessions. I would jog into the waiting room with color on my cheeks and sometimes even with a racquet in hand. Other times, I would show up straight from a lovely lunch out with friends.

I knew I was putting on an act, but I felt great and lots of people told me I looked healthy, too. This inspired me and made me feel better, and so the upward spiral continued.

In hindsight, I think I can say that my good mood (which I had to work *really* hard to achieve) was an important part of my recovery. It's devastating to you and those around you when you fall into a deep depression during your illness. Sooner or later, your friends will start to pull away from you.

Nobody wants to talk about illness, especially not anyone else's.

Remember that the answer to the greeting: "How are you doing?" is always "Fine, thank you."

Unfortunately, there are plenty of old people who break this basic rule. Impulse control is equally important when you're old!

102

STOP
FEELING
GUILTY

I have arrhythmia—irregular heart rhythm—because of a bad bout of double-sided pneumonia I got in New York that I didn't nurse well enough. Even though I wasn't feeling well, I worked every day and biked through Central Park. It was completely my own fault and I've stopped feeling guilty about it. Doing so would just make me feel even more sick. With today's medications, arrhythmia can be treated easily and the prescribed lifestyle is simple enough to follow.

I've also taught myself a few tricks for calming myself down. They usually work. Find your own ways to calm yourself. It's actually pretty useful knowledge to have, since you can also use it in other circumstances as well.

103

STAY AS ACTIVE
AS YOU CAN

Recently, it became more and more difficult
to walk and sleep because of pains in my legs
and hips. It turned out that I had osteoarthritis
and needed to have surgery, which I immediately
agreed to. Within three months, I had a new hip
made out of titanium—the word alone makes me
happy!—and now I can walk without any limp-
ing or pain. I actually walk faster than I have in
years, because now I walk to stay in shape.

It's amazing how many spare parts there are
out there for humans!

A hip replacement is a big but routine operation, but it does require a lot from the patient. You
have to perform small exercises constantly—but

never too many at a time. And "You're the one who has to do them, not me!"—as my physical therapist shrugged when I wanted to schedule more appointments.

I had to sacrifice my squash games and going ice-skating—two big losses for me that I replaced with golf (the perfect sport for people with hip replacements). But I feel incredibly lucky that I'm able to move about without any pain. Biking, walking, and cross-country skiing is more fun than ever now that I realize it's something I shouldn't take for granted.

And on top of that, I can continue to be active and keep in shape. To be in good physical condition is a great advantage when big illnesses affect you. But don't forget that your fitness is only as good as your current routine. I was happy to note during a hospital test in 2013 that my physical condition was 20 percent better than in 2004 despite having aged nearly ten years. Hopefully, it is the same with my brain-power!

You have to keep working on yourself all the time. There's no way around it.

104

CONFRONT YOUR ILLNESSES RIGHT AWAY

This might seem like an obvious statement, and it is when it comes to cancer. But it's not so obvious when it comes to osteoarthritis in your hips and knees, because many people fear surgery or think they're just too old to undergo any kind of invasive procedure.

This is incomprehensible to me! That attitude means that sooner or later you'll end up handicapped, and you won't be able to walk without assistance—not to mention the other things you'll have to give up. It's simply a way to give up on yourself, marginalizing and ending your life ahead of your time.

We have to believe that there's always one more good reason to keep going just a little bit longer. As long as we can make our own decisions, there's no good alternative to being healthy. That's why we always have to take a chance on the surgeries that can restore our former abilities and keep us going.

105

BUILD
A MEMORY
PALACE

Many treatments and operations are unpleasant and can take a long time. I know, because I've been through several. You're stuck on a gurney for hours and it's easy to let your imagination run wild. If there's ever a time to use self-hypnosis to keep calm, this is it.

During ancient times, it was considered a sport to build memory palaces, used to find out how much a person could remember. Homer knew *The Iliad* and *The Odyssey* by heart. At a time without any hard drives, this was a great challenge. During my illnesses, this ancient technique was a pastime of mine, and it gave me much pleasure.

This is how it's done:

When I'm lying there on the gurney waiting for my treatment or operation, I'm deprived of everything.

This is when I use the memory palace technique. I close my eyes and go back to my childhood home in Uppsala.

Slowly and methodically, I reconstruct the house in the utmost detail and walk through each room to take inventory of the things inside. *Nothing* should be left out; *everything* has to be accounted for, even the contents of the drawers and closets. But you have to be strict with yourself if this is going to work. If you're not, the self-hypnosis won't go into effect.

You can actually remember almost everything when you're lying down on a hospital gurney.

Just to make sure that I'm not interrupted by the doctors or nurses, I always bring an eye mask with me. When my eyes are covered, I can concentrate completely and am even able to forget where I am, though I can feel what they are doing to me. But at that point, I simply don't care because I'm completely occupied.

This method works so well that I've never managed to complete any of these inventories.

"You're all finished now!" someone will suddenly say, just as I've located the aluminum pressure cooker in the left kitchen cabinet of my childhood home in 1953.

"Already?" I ask brightly and look up for the first time, since I've been somewhere completely different.

I'll have been on that gurney for three hours and haven't even been a little concerned.

That's how many of us have the power to "self-hypnotize." It is a real boon to be able to do this, and it keeps you in good spirits. And therefore, I wish with all my heart that you too can build your own memory palace.

106

IT'S NOT
AS BAD AS
YOU THINK

"It's not that bad," my wife usually says. "The worst thing that can happen is that you die."

These days, I completely agree. It's a good way to master your feelings. After all, what can I do if the social security system collapses or a pandemic hits us? Not much. Each generation usually experiences one large traumatic event.

When I was about to undergo my first cardio-version in New York, I remember—just as the anesthesia was taking effect and I thought I was going to die—my last thought was, very calmly:

"At least now I don't have to deal with the IRS anymore."

107

DON'T PICTURE
DEATH EVERYWHERE

As my American doctor said, "For my patients, death isn't an option."

That's an exaggeration, but the attitude can still be of undeniable help in difficult situations. Believing that everything will work out is half the battle. Certain lies do make you feel better.

108

YOU'RE THE ONE WHO HAS TO LIVE YOUR OWN LIFE

The more illnesses you experience, the thicker your skin grows, and your will to live is enforced. We're meant to live life in the best way possible and maintain our good humor. That's the simple answer to the timeless question of the meaning of life.

Life goes up and life goes down. Cherish the highs, the love, the children, waking up in a tent at sunrise among thousands of wild animals in the African savannah, finding Robert Frost's cabin in Breadloaf, Vermont, or the memory of the tinkle of sheep bells on Odysseus's home island Ithaca, where a friend recited Homer from memory.

109

REST IN PEACE

This is my last piece of advice. Everyone has their own Elysium. Mine is Kivik, Österlen, in the south of Sweden. It's my country's answer to Provence, where the sea, the beaches, the hills, and everything else is endless. But only five hundred yards inland, the landscape becomes lush and hilly, dotted with small villages of timbered houses and surrounded by apple groves.

Remnants of the Stone and Bronze Ages can be found all around. People have lived in this spot for many thousands of years and left behind memories of themselves and their lives.

My family comes here every summer. My children learned to ride their bicycles among the

Viking graves. It gives us a thousand-year perspective of life on Earth. The seasons come and go. In this landscape I have found the peace of mind I was so often lacking. This is where I hope one day to rest.